GW00775639

SEMAPHORE ALPHABET

& NUMERICAL SIGNS

The Naval & Military Press Ltd

Published by

The Naval & Military Press Ltd
Unit 5 Riverside, Brambleside
Bellbrook Industrial Estate
Uckfield, East Sussex
TN22 1QQ England

Tel: +44 (0)1825 749494

www.naval-military-press.com
www.nmarchive.com

SEMAPHORE SIGNALLING

In the field this simple means of signalling is usefully employed at short distances such as between columns and their advanced or rear guards, across rivers, defiles, or fire swept zones, and to connect an attacking line with its supports.

The following points must be carefully attended to both at drill and when actually sending messages:

(1) The Signaller must stand exactly facing the station he is sending to.
(2) The flags must not be thrown to the rear and must be held at the full extent of the arms and in exact prolongation of them.
(3) The arms must be placed at the exact positions indicating the letters, signs, etc.
(4) When making the letters T, O, W, and the numeral sign, the flags must be separated and not covering one another.
(5) The Signaller must turn slightly on the hips wen making such letters as I, X, etc., but the eyes must continue to look straight to the front.
(6) When double letters occur the flags are to be brought well into the body after the first letter is made.
(7) The flags are to be kept unfurled and to be moved quickly from one letter or sign to the next; a pause is to be made on the letter or sign according to the rate of sending.
(8) When sending is going on, everyone except the Signaller must stand clear of the flags.
(9) Both flags must be of the same colour.

The simplest method of learning the alphabet and the other signs is by circles, thus:

1st Circle – A to G

2nd Circle – H to N

3rd Circle – O to S

4th Circle – T, U, Y, and "ERASE"

5th Circle – "Numeral Sign," "J"
                   (or "Alphabet Sign" and V

6th Circle – W and X, and

7th Circle – Z

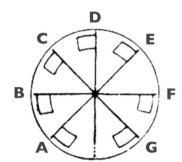

At Drill in the first circle, the letters A to D will be made with the right arm and E to G with the left.

When not at drill the letters should be formed with the arms in the most convenient manner, but in making letters where only one arm is used, that arm should not be brought across the body.

When letters follow one another as in a word or group, the flags will not be brought back to the ready after each letter, but if an arm is already in position to form or assist to form the next, it will be kept steady.

When sending words, groups etc., the arms are moved from letter to letter and are both brought on to the non-signalling position on completion of the word.

The caller and writer should stand immediately in rear of the sender and reader respectively, so that they may be clear of the flags and yet close enough to be heard and to hear the latter distinctively.

The same signs are used for the numerals 1 to 0 as for the letters A to K (omitting J) but are distinguished from the latter by being preceded by the "numeral sign" (equivalent to the F.1. on the Morse system) and followed by the "alphabetical sign" (equivalent to F.F. on the Morse system). They are checked by being repeated back.
The Stop Signal is "P.P.".

The "General Answer" is "T" (one dash) made as in Morse.

The Preparative is "J" and waving the flags, and is answered by the "General Answer".

Known stations are called up and answer by their station calls; unknown stations by the "Preparative" and answered by the "General Answer".

The "Erase" (opposite to L) is used (a) to erase a word or a group sent incorrectly; or (b) to erase a word or a group incorrectly checked.

READY.

NUMERICAL SIGN.

ERASE.

J

ALPHABETICAL SIGN.

B 2

C   3

D 4

E

5

F   6

H 8

K   O

L

M

P

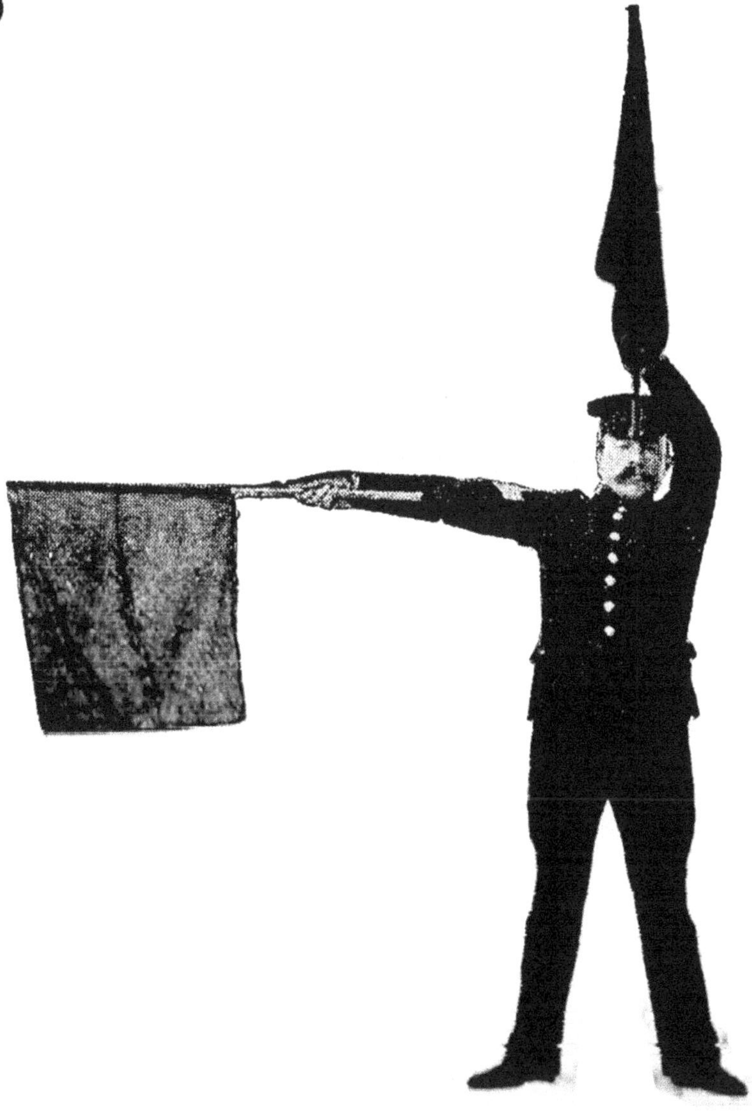

Q

R

R

S

T

U

V

W

X

z

Lightning Source UK Ltd.
Milton Keynes UK
UKHW030627080321
379980UK00010B/1604